A Year of
Buddhist Festivals

Flora York

W
FRANKLIN WATTS
LONDON•SYDNEY

This edition 2013

First published by Franklin Watts

Copyright © 2008 Franklin Watts

Franklin Watts
338 Euston Road
London NW1 3BH

Franklin Watts Australia
Level 17/207 Kent Street
Sydney NSW 2000

Dewey classification: 294.3'436
ISBN: 978 1 4451 1783 6

Art Direction: Jonathan Hair   Designer (original edition): Joelle Wheelwright
Illustrations: Peter Bull   Picture Research: Diana Morris
Faith Consultant: Munisha, Education Officer, The Clear Vision Trust

Produced for Franklin Watts by Storeybooks. The text of this book is based on
Buddhist Festivals Through the Year by Anita Ganeri © Franklin Watts 2003.

Acknowledgements
The publishers would like to thank the following for permission to reproduce
photographs in this book: David Cummings/ Eye Ubiquitous: 6, 21b; John Dakers/
Eye Ubiquitous: 14; Nick Dawson/ World Religions Photo Library: 24, 25t; Bennett
Dean/ Eye Ubiquitous: 7b; A. Deutsch/ Trip: 11; Gapper/ World Religions Photo
Library: 8, 22; C. McCooey/ Trip: 26; Christine Osborne/ World Religions Photo
Library: 10, 13, 16b, 18b, 19, 20t, 20b; Tim Page/ Eye Ubiquitous: front cover, 12,
16t, 18t; H. Rogers/Trip: 17; Paul Seheult/ Eye Ubiquitous: 7t; Pam Smith/ Eye
Ubiquitous: 23; Superbild/ A1pix: 15; A. Tovey/ Trip: 27b; Julia Waterlow/ Eye
Ubiquitous: 9, 25b. Every attempt has been made to clear copyright. Should there be
any inadvertent omission please apply to the publisher for rectification.

Printed in China

Franklin Watts is a division of Hachette Children's Books,
an Hachette UK company.
www.hachette.co.uk

Contents

Words printed in **bold** are explained in the glossary.

Buddhists

About 2,500 years ago, a man called Siddhattha Gotama lived in India. He became known as the Buddha. People who follow his teachings are called Buddhists.

There are about 400 million Buddhists in the world today. Their religion is called Buddhism.

A Buddhist monk. ▶

Buddhism today

- Buddhism is the main religion in Sri Lanka and Thailand.
- In North America and Europe, Buddhism is also popular.
- There are not many Buddhists in India, where Buddhism began.

Life of the Buddha

Siddhattha Gotama was the son of a king. One day he saw a **monk**, who seemed happy although he had nothing. Siddhattha decided to live like the monk did, and try to find why people feel unhappy and how they could be helped.

After many years, he understood why people feel unhappy. He travelled around India, teaching people what he had learned.

Being a Buddhist

Buddhists do not see the Buddha as God. They **worship** him as a very special human, and show their respect in various ways. They put **offerings** of flowers, incense and candles in front of statues of the Buddha. They **chant** verses from **sacred** writings.

*A Buddhist **shrine** ▶ in Thailand.*

The Noble Eightfold Path

Buddha said that the way to be happy in life is to do these eight things.

▼ *This wheel **symbolises** the Eightfold Path.*

1. **Understand the Buddha's teachings.**
2. **Follow the Buddha's teachings.**
3. **Speak kindly and truthfully.**
4. **Be generous.**
5. **Do a job that does not harm others.**
6. **Always try your best.**
7. **Be alert and aware.**
8. **Train your mind to be calm.**

Buddhist groups

There are different groups of Buddhists, which look at the Buddha's teachings in slightly different ways.

The two main groups are called Theravada and Mahayana.

Buddhists live all over the world, and Buddhist festivals may be slightly different in each country.

▲ *Giving gifts to the monks in a monastery in London, England.*

Buddhist festivals

A festival is a special time when people gather together to mark or **celebrate** an event.

Some festivals last for a day; others last for several days. Each festival has its own **customs** and **ceremonies**. These may take place at home, at a **temple** or **monastery**, or in towns and villages.

Some Buddhist festivals are celebrated by all Buddhists. Others are special to certain groups.

Different Buddhists

These are some of the different Buddhist groups.

Theravada Buddhists
• They follow the Buddha's teachings very closely.
• They live mainly in Sri Lanka, Myanmar, Thailand, Cambodia and Laos.

Mahayana Buddhists
• They live mainly in Nepal, China, Japan, Korea and Vietnam.
• They believe in many different buddhas.

Tibetan Buddhists
• They come from Tibet. Their leader is called the Dalai Lama.
• They follow Mahayana Buddhism mixed with later teachings.

Friends of the Western Buddhist Order
• A Buddhist group started by Sangharakshita in Britain in 1967. He wanted a new style of Buddhism that was suitable for people in **Western** countries, where Buddhism was new and there were few monks and nuns.

Full Moon Days

Early Buddhists did not have clocks or diaries, so they met on days when there was a full moon. Today, many Buddhist festivals still take place on these days. In the **West**, the nearest weekend may be used instead.

Acting out Buddhist stories. ▶

Wesak

The festival of *Wesak* is in April or May. This is a very important time for Theravada Buddhists. They remember three things: Buddha's birthday, enlightenment (see page 11) and death. Mahayana Buddhists celebrate these three events on separate days.

At *Wesak*, Buddhists try to be especially kind, generous and caring towards others.

▲ *A painting showing the moment when the Buddha was enlightened.*

Nirvana

The Buddha taught people the way to reach nirvana. Nirvana is a way of feeling. It means you feel perfectly peaceful and kind.

For Buddhists to reach nirvana, it is important to follow the Noble Eightfold Path (see page 7). This guide helps them to learn the right way to live.

Buddhists gradually learn to be happy with their life. Instead of always thinking about themselves and the things that they want, they try to help other people.

Buddha dies

When the Buddha was about to die, he told his monks not to be sad. He reminded them of his teaching that everything changes and passes away. He told the monks to carry on spreading his teachings to people.

▼ *This huge statue in Sri Lanka shows Buddha at the end of his life.*

The three events of Wesak

Buddha's birthday
Siddhattha Gotama (the Buddha) was born in India in about 480 BCE.

Buddha's enlightenment
When Siddhattha was a young man, he decided to live as a monk and try and find answers to his questions about life. He spent many years doing this, but finally he had the answers. Buddhists say that he gained enlightenment. 'Buddha' means 'enlightened one'. That is how Siddhattha got his new name.

Buddha's death
The Buddha died when he was about 80 years old.

Celebrating Wesak

Many Buddhists go to monasteries at *Wesak* and take gifts for the monks and **nuns**. Being generous is very important to Buddhists. They also place offerings in front of a statue of the Buddha in the shrine room.

The monks give talks about the Buddha's life. There is a special ceremony for *Wesak*.

Lighting oil lamps to celebrate ▶
Wesak in Sri Lanka.

Honouring the Buddha

Buddhists place offerings in front of an image of the Buddha. Each has a special meaning:
• Oil lamps, lanterns or candles stand for the Buddha's wisdom (knowledge, experience and understanding).

• Flowers look beautiful but soon die. This reminds Buddhists that nothing lasts for ever.
• Incense has a sweet smell and is a reminder of the goodness of the Buddha's teachings.

Wesak lights

In Sri Lanka, people decorate their homes with lanterns or candles. There are big displays in the streets.

Lights are symbols of the Buddha's enlightenment. They are like the Buddha's teachings – Buddhists think these light up the world.

In Thailand, there is a candlelit procession around the temple at the end of *Wesak*.

▲ *Bright lanterns mark the Buddha's birthday.*

Jataka stories

At *Wesak*, children listen to *Jataka* stories about the Buddha.

In one story, the Buddha is born as a lion. One day, a jackal saves the lion's life, so in return he protects him and helps him to find food. This story teaches that it is good to have friends, and important to help people.

Wesak card

Make a card to send at *Wesak*.

Decorate it with a picture of the Buddha, or a **lotus** blossom. Write 'Happy *Wesak*' inside.

O-bon

This Mahayana Buddhist festival takes place in Japan in July or August. Families remember their **ancestors** who have died.

They believe that at *O-bon*, the **spirits** of the dead come to visit them. This is not scary or sad – *O-bon* is a very happy festival.

▲ *A traditional folk dance for* O-bon.

The story behind O-bon

Maudgalyayana was one of the Buddha's chief followers. His mother died and her spirit felt very bad because of a lie she had told. Maudgalyayana could feel how sad she was. Only the Buddha could help her. So Maudgalyayana gave a feast as an offering to the Buddha. Then the mother's spirit became happy again.

Celebrations

On the first day of the festival, people decorate their houses with lanterns, put flowers on the family shrine, and light small bonfires to welcome the spirits home.

On the second day, there is a feast in the village, with dancing and games.

On the third day, people make offerings at their family shrine, and ask the Buddha to **bless** their ancestors. Then they believe that the spirits leave. Buddhist monks visit as many homes as they can during *O-bon*.

▼ *Lights ready for sailing on a river.*

Floating lights

People make tiny boats from paper or straw, and put a candle inside. They push them out on to lakes and rivers to carry the spirits back to their world at the end of *O-bon*.

Make your own lights – float tea-lights on a bowl of water. (Do not leave burning if you are not in the room.)

Poson

Poson is a festival celebrated by Theravada Buddhists from Sri Lanka. It reminds Buddhists of when Buddhism came to Sri Lanka.

The story behind Poson

The Sri Lankan king asked the emperor of India to send a monk to teach him about Buddhism. After listening to the monk, the king became a Buddhist.

In Sri Lanka there are processions for *Poson*, telling the story of the king and Buddhism. Sri Lankans who live in the West go to the temple.

Tree of wisdom

The Buddha was sitting under a tree when he became enlightened. It is now called the *Bodhi* tree. The word '*bodhi*' means 'wisdom' or 'enlightenment'. A cutting from the tree was taken to Sri Lanka and planted in Anuradhapura, where it grew into a new tree. Buddhist **pilgrims** visit this very **holy** place.

◀ *The* Bodhi *tree in Anuradhapura.*

Asala

The festival of *Asala* remembers the first teaching that the Buddha gave after his enlightenment.

▼ *Sarnath, India. Buddha first taught people here.*

The Wheel of Law

The Buddha's first teaching was called the Turning of the Wheel of Law. He taught that life is a continuous cycle of change. The cells in our bodies grow, die and are renewed. Our feelings can change from worry to happiness.

We are learning about life all the time, and so we can change ourselves to become better people. This is a kind of rebirth. Following the Noble Eightfold Path (see page 7) is the way to live a kind, peaceful and happy life.

Asala processions

In Kandy, Sri Lanka, there are processions to celebrate *Asala*. Over 100 elephants, dancers, drummers and acrobats parade through the streets.

One of the Buddha's teeth is kept in a casket in the Temple of the Tooth. Every day, people **honour** this **relic**.

In the procession, an elephant carries a copy of the casket on its back.

▲ *The elephants in the procession wear decorated cloths.*

◄ *A dancer with the elephant procession.*

The Four Noble Truths

The Buddha said that there were four truths about life that people needed to understand.

1. Everyone's life is unpleasant sometimes.
2. If you always want things, you will never be happy.
3. It is possible to stop wanting things.
4. The way to become happy is to follow the Noble Eightfold Path (see page 7).

Kathina

Kathina is a Theravada Buddhist festival. Buddhists visit monasteries to give new robes to the monks at a special ceremony.

▼ *The Buddha and his monks.*

How Kathina began

The rainy season made it hard for the Buddha and his monks to travel around and teach. They stayed in a monastery until the weather got better. Another group of monks was planning to join the Buddha in the monastery. But the rains started early and they could not go. The Buddha told them to sew a new robe for one of the monks. He knew that this would cheer them up.

A new robe

At the *Kathina* ceremony, cloth for a robe is given to the monks. They decide which monk needs it most. The cloth is given to thank the monks for living a holy life that is a good example for people to follow.

In Thailand, the celebrations for *Kathina* last for a week. During this time, the king visits nine monasteries, giving the monks new *Kathina* robes.

▲ *Buddhist monks in their robes.*

◀ *At* Kathina, *people pin offerings of money to a model tree.*

Buddhist promises

All Buddhists make five promises. They *will not*:
- Harm living things.
- Take anything that is not freely given.
- Misuse their senses.
- Speak wrongly.
- Use drugs or drink alcohol.

Buddhist monks and nuns make five extra promises. They *will not*:
- Eat after midday.
- Sing or dance.
- Use perfume or cosmetics.
- Sleep in a soft bed.
- Handle money.

Monks and nuns

Some Buddhists decide to become a monk or a nun. They go to live in a monastery (or **nunnery**) and lead a very simple life. They study holy writings, **meditate**, run the monastery and help local people to lead better lives.

In some countries, monks rely on local people to give them food to eat.

People can put gifts into a monk's alms bowl.

▼ *Boys dressed for a ceremony before they become monks.*

A monk's possessions

The Buddha said that monks were only allowed to own eight things. These are:
1. Robes.
2. Belt.
3. Needle and thread.
4. Alms bowl.
5. Walking stick.
6. Razor.
7. Toothpick.
8. Water filter.

Alms bowl

Robes

Razor

Sangha Day

On *Sangha* Day, Buddhists give thanks for the love and friendship that they share with other Buddhists. This is one of the Friends of the Western Buddhist Order's main festivals.

Celebrations

In the West, Buddhists may meet in a Buddhist centre or a temple. On Sangha Day, they may go there to meet their friends.

In the shrine room, people sit in front of the image of the Buddha and chant or meditate. They celebrate their community of Buddhist friends and teachers. They may listen to a talk.

▲ *A Buddhist man lights a candle at a Buddhist centre in London, England.*

A way of life

Buddhists know that Buddhism will help them to deal with any problems in their lives.

They often chant the following words:

'I go to the Buddha as my refuge.
I go to the *Dharma* as my refuge.
I go to the *Sangha* as my refuge.'

• A refuge is a place where you can feel safe and happy.
• *Dharma* means 'the Buddha's teachings'.
• *Sangha* means 'the Buddhist community'.

Losar

The festival of *Losar* is in February, and marks the Tibetan New Year. It is celebrated by Tibetan Buddhists. *Losar* lasts for several days.

▼ *Prayer flags on a Tibetan Buddhist temple.*

Prayers and offerings

People visit temples at *Losar* to honour the Buddha. They give *khatas* (white greeting scarves) and food to the monks. The monks chant from the sacred texts.

In Tibet, coloured prayer flags are flown on temples and homes. These have hundreds of prayers written on them. The prayer flags stay up for a year and are replaced at the next *Losar*.

New year celebrations

Losar is the time to make a new start for the year to come. Homes are cleaned and decorated, and people have new clothes to wear.

It is a happy occasion. People visit their family and friends, and any quarrels are settled. They also think about the Buddha.

A special dance

In Tibet, the *Cham* dance may be performed at festivals. This special dance is all about good winning out over evil. Dancers dress as good or evil characters, such as the skeleton lords. The dance is meant to frighten away evil spirits and make sure that the new year starts well.

▼ *A* Cham *dancer in Tibet.*

Butter sculptures

Monks make offerings called *tormas*. These are dough covered with sculptures made from yak butter. Some of the decorations are lucky symbols. There are also scenes to show the Buddha's life.

Try making a 'butter sculpture' using modelling clay or plasticine. Shape it into flowers, the sun or the moon. Leave the sculpture to dry until it is hard, then decorate it with paint or glitter.

▲ *A monk making a butter sculpture for* Losar.

Dumplings

There is special dumpling soup to eat at *Losar*. The dumplings have things hidden inside to show what the new year will bring. Coal means a bad year ahead. Salt means good luck.

Tibetan Buddhists ▶ *making cakes for* Losar.

Throwing flour

Tibetans eat a lot of *tsampa* (barley flour). When you visit someone's home at *Losar*, you are given a pot of *tsampa*. You throw a bit into the air to honour the Buddha and to bring good luck. People also throw *tsampa* at the temples.

Hana-Matsuri

In Japan, *Hana-Matsuri* is a very important festival. Mahayana Buddhists celebrate the Buddha's birthday at this time.

The Buddha is born

Buddhists tell this story about Buddha's birth. When it was time for him to be born, his mother set off to her parents' house. On the way she stopped in a garden full of flowers, where birds sang. Then she had her baby, and bathed him in perfumed water.

Flower festival

'*Hana-Matsuri*' means 'flower festival'. It takes place in April, when the cherry trees are covered in beautiful flowers. The cherry blossom is Japan's special flower. The delicate blossoms only last for a short time. This reminds people about one of the Buddha's teachings – that everything changes.

Children wear flowers in their hair at *Hana-Matsuri.* People hang streamers in the streets to look like cherry blossom.

▲ *A lantern for* Hana-Matsuri *near a cherry blossom tree.*

Make cherry blossom

You will need:

Twigs
Small circles of pink or
  white tissue paper

1. Fold the circles into four.
Twist into flower shapes.

2. Stick the paper
blossoms on the twigs.

Celebrating Hana-Matsuri

There are special events at the temple at *Hana-Matsuri*. A model of the flower garden where the Buddha was born is set up outside. Visitors spoon a special hydrangea-leaf tea over a model baby Buddha. It smells nice and is like the water that the newborn Buddha was bathed in.

There are storytellers, acrobats and dancers to watch. You can buy fish soup, rice balls, paper umbrellas and lucky charms.

▼ *Storytellers for Hana-Matsuri.*

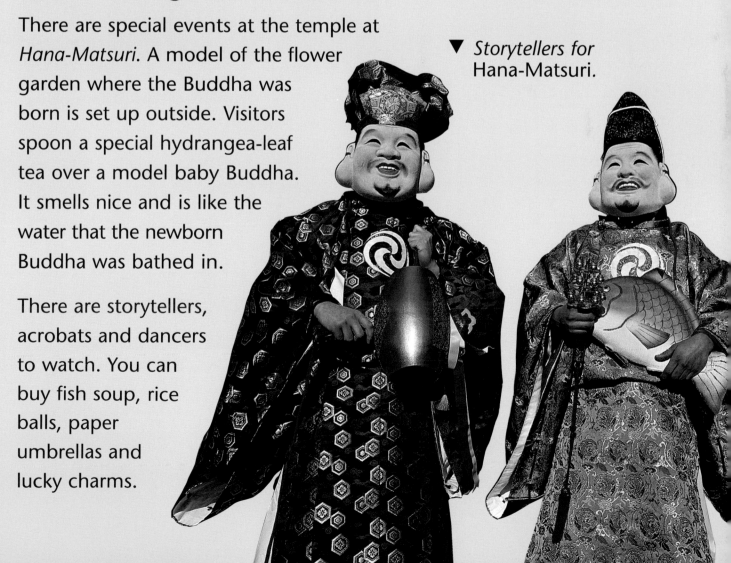

Festival calendar

Month	Festival
April/May	*Wesak* (Theravada)
July/August	*O-bon* (Mahayana/Japan)
June/July	*Poson* (Theravada)
July/August	*Asala* (Theravada)
October/November	*Kathina* (Theravada)
November	*Sangha* Day (FWBO)
February	*Losar* (Tibet)
April	*Hana-Matsuri* (Mahayana/Japan)

Buddhist months

In Pali, an ancient Indian language, the months of the Buddhist **lunar year** are:

Citta	(March/April)
Vesaka	(April/May)
Jettha	(May/June)
Asalha	(June/July)
Savana	(July/August)
Potthabada	(August/September)
Assayuja	(September/October)
Kattika	(October/November)
Maggasira	(November/December)
Pussa	(December/January)
Maga	(January/February)
Phagguna	(February/March)

Glossary

Ancestors   People in your family who lived before you.

Bless   For Buddhists, to say special words of blessing that give good wishes to someone or something.

Celebrate   To be pleased and happy about something, and to have special festivities, or celebrations, to mark the occasion.

Ceremonies   Occasions where you do special things to mark an event.

Chant   To half-speak, half-sing sacred writings.

Customs   Habits or traditions.

Holy   Something sacred (see below). A person who is holy is extremely kind, wise, and devoted to religion and the god or person he or she honours.

Honour   To show great respect by saying special words or making offerings.

Lotus   A flower that grows in ponds. For Buddhists, it is a symbol of enlightenment.

Lunar year   A calendar based on the position of the moon. A lunar year has 354 days.

Meditate   To relax the body and the mind, especially as a religious act.

Monastery   A place where monks live, work and study.

Monk; nun   People who give up their home and belongings to follow a religious way of life. A monk is a man; a nun is a woman.

Nunnery   A place where nuns live, work and study.

Offerings   Things that are given as a mark of respect.

Pilgrims   People who make a special journey to a sacred place, such as a temple or monastery. This is called a pilgrimage.

Relic   Something that once belonged to a holy person.

Sacred   Something very special and important that is connected to a religion or a god. It is given great respect.

Shrine   A place that is linked to a sacred person, object or god. You go there to honour or worship that person. Buddhists honour the Buddha.

Spirits   Sometimes people use the word 'spirit' to describe a person's consciousness, or awareness, which carries on after the body has died.

Symbolises   Stands for something else.

Temple   For Buddhists, a building where they go to worship the Buddha.

West; Western   'The West' is countries of the Western world, such as Europe and the USA.

Worship   To show great love and respect for someone. In a religion, this can include singing hymns, saying prayers, reading sacred writings and making offerings.

Further resources

Websites

www.buddhanet.net/e-learning/buddhism/index.htm
Buddhist stories, crafts and activities.

www.thegrid.org.uk/learning/re/virtual/buddhisttrail/index.shtml
Visit a Buddhist monastery.

www.clear-vision.org/Students/underEleven.aspx
Stories and games about the Buddha.

www.bbc.co.uk/religion/galleries/sandmandala
Pictures showing the making of a mandala (special Buddhist art).

Note to parents and teachers: Every effort has been made by the Publishers to ensure that these websites are suitable for children, that they are of the highest educational value, and that they contain no inappropriate or offensive material. However, because of the nature of the Internet, it is impossible to guarantee that the contents of these sites will not be altered. We strongly advise that Internet access is supervised by a responsible adult.

Index